Creating Home

Design for Living

Creating Home
Design for Living

KEITH SUMMEROUR
WRITTEN WITH MARC KRISTAL

RIZZOLI
NEW YORK

New York · Paris · London · Milan

I would like to dedicate
this book to my forefathers
and their pursuit of
architecture. As I travel
the world in discovery of
their efforts I am reminded
of the mountain of works
from which I benefit daily.

We live in the most amazing
time of all times, a world
of communication and
ideas, of planes and
instant Internet research.
This time will be known
as the age of creativity.
For this I am thankful to be
able to work and build
upon the labors of the ages.

CONTENTS

INTRODUCTION

I believe it reasonable to say that drawing—which is, of course, an essential component of my profession, even as it becomes something of a lost art—has always been as meaningful to my creative existence as architecture. And like many able amateurs, I have sought to learn from my betters. One from whom I have gotten a great deal is John Singer Sargent—not so much the penetrating portraits for which he is justly remembered, but rather his masterful landscape and genre sketches, works that were often swiftly executed and are consequently more immediate. For these pictures, Sargent used a technique I particularly admire: he would draw a certain element in great detail, then let its surroundings fall into an impressionistic soft focus—enabling the viewer to complete the sketch based on his or her response to what Sargent had provided. Thus did the beholder finish what the artist began; together, they became cocreators of the artwork.

Inspired by Sargent, I myself have come to leave a degree of white (or, latterly, gray) space on the page when I draw. And I have migrated the lesson into architecture: as a designer of houses, it has become my main premise that I need to leave part of a building open to interpretation, to enable the people using it to bring to the canvas of home that which they already carry within.

In this way does one become open to seeing a building—a house—from a different, unexpected perspective. And from there, to asking the critical question: What is it that truly adds value to one's life?

Though it is perhaps not my place to do so, I counsel my clients to try to draw a distinction between how they think they *want* to live versus how they actually *do* live. Many of us, when we contemplate building a dream home, carry an ideal in our minds that involves lifestyle moments we have seen in other people's abodes (in real life, or on TV or in the movies) that we think we might like to emulate. I'm not making a judgment on this; we are all susceptible to it. Still, before design development begins, I ask people to consider their daily experiences, because the activities requiring a bit of extra effort can be the ones that, consciously or otherwise, you most appreciate. Making coffee, for example: You go into the kitchen, you need to get down the grinder and filter and measure out the beans, and do the slow pour once the water's boiled to extract the optimum flavor. You're not always in the mood. But you lay hands on your morning tools, and take the trouble to get the brew just so, and get the day going with craft and finesse and grace. Whereas in your dream house, you come into the kitchen, push a stainless steel button—and out comes a cappuccino without the slightest effort on your part at all. Which cup is the more satisfying?

Maybe it's a Southern thing, and maybe it isn't. But I have always felt that working for some aspect of one's daily experience is one of life's great joys. Gardening exemplifies this—you put in a little work, and up come the tomatoes and herbs and flowers. But that effort can be as simple as how you fill your bathtub, or the way you lay out your clothes or skim the leaves from the water's surface before taking a morning swim. These rituals, which compel us to grind the gears a bit to achieve satisfaction, give texture and character and soul to our days—and tend to be the first things erased when we fantasize about how we imagine we'd like to live.

Am I suggesting that when people entrust me with the design of large, lavish, and expensive houses—typically second homes, *dream* homes—I tell them to learn to coexist with imperfection? Not at all: I respect and honor the wishes of my clients completely. Rather, I mean that embracing a great idea all but ensures a great house, and it is in learning to live with the quirks the idea produces that we make the house our own. "First thought, best thought," the poet Allen Ginsberg often declared, and I concur: some of the most successful projects I've done have been conceived in a very short period of time, even a matter of hours. Though the core idea gets refined over the course of construction, it isn't overthought or questioned, and it remains so strong that the end users are willing to overlook any adjustments it might necessitate down the line.

My own country house is just such a place. It takes the form of a five-story stone tower, and the master bedroom, which occupies the entirety of the third floor, has thirty-mile views on three sides and superlative natural ventilation. The bathroom, alas, is down two flights. I'd prefer it to be en suite, but not so much that I would sacrifice the exquisite feelings of gratitude and well-being that flood me each morning when I consider my surroundings. Instead, I have learned to adjust myself to my home's personality, just as I might accept the quirks of a special, appealingly complicated friend.

Arriving at this perspective was not automatic, but derived from a journey that also involved drawing—one that led me away from the constricting rigor of the line to the pleasurable ambiguity of form. This required a leap of faith, for an architect is trained to see the world through the line; it comes to represent detail, fit, and finish, an ideal of perfection and symmetry. Some six years ago, I took a sabbatical, moving to Italy to take drawing lessons at the Florence Academy of Art, and the first thing I had to overcome was the architect's habit of using lines to make a sketch. I needed to push myself to see in form, which is, of course, how we all experience the world. It was a difficult transition. But once I'd trained my hand to "think" in shapes, in light and shade and shadow, I became more cognizant of texture and depth, elements that opened the way to a deeper understanding of architecture than I had previously experienced.

My transition to form remains a work in progress. But it has improved everything about my practice. And I have benefited from a simple willingness to let go: to be released from the old, comfortable paradigms and venture into the unknown. It opened the way for me not only to think differently, but to entertain a whole new way of looking at life, one that deeply enriched my craft—an exercise that can be of benefit to anyone, especially when undertaking the creation of a house.

It was while I was in Italy as well that I began to understand the importance of not over-finishing a project, paradoxically through the study of repurposed structures in which, by inclination and sometimes by code, architects left something of the historic life of the buildings on view, so that the modern-day visitor might perceive their souls. *Palimpsest*—an object in which multiple layers of history can be grasped—has become an overused word in my profession. Yet it is an important one, because the idea of things coexisting—of being able to look through the present reality of a building to the record of its earlier habitations—mirrors the way in which we experience reality. *Life* is a palimpsest, in which, beat by beat, we inhabit not only the living moment, but also all of the memories and associations that hover behind it.

Travel is perhaps our greatest ally in this regard. The grand tour of yesteryear, which was the exclusive province of individuals of wealth and privilege, is now something that can be experienced and enjoyed by many; the pool of memories and associations is wider and deeper than it was for our grandparents. Increasingly, the people for whom I design houses possess knowledge drawn from travel, unconscious impressions that flicker to life when they see the schemes I've crafted. This is the highest achievement to which I can aspire: the creation of houses for people that are so in tune with who they are that they become magnets for their entire histories—houses that are summations of their memories and experiences, and gateways to all that is to come. Thus does the white space of a home fulfill a double function: as a zone in which to locate the past and to build the future.

Though I am speaking of white space, I should add that nowadays I sketch on gray paper. Form is important, but so is texture: a black line on a white sheet is harsh, but if you apply dark graphite to a light gray page, the edge becomes malleable and more is left to the imagination. In discussing drawing, one often talks about the soft edge, and that translates, in architecture, into comfort, into materials that are embracing actually and experientially. A reclaimed-timber floor, let us say, will exude a warmth and softness that is easier on the spirit than the machined edge of modernity, and the heel marks and natural craquelure suggest the comfort of tradition and history. The texture of material becomes the texture of life: enriched by education, anecdote, and all else that we bring to it.

Most enriching of all is the process of collaboration. The architect does not engage only with the page, but also with the site; the climate, history, and tradition; the availability of materials; the client or clients; and the extraordinary talents that bring a house, in all of its complexity, to life. Just as an author may not entirely understand what has been put on a page until a readership has responded, I can't quite take the full measure of an idea until it has been tested by a project's landscape architect and interior designer, and even the builder, artists, and craftspeople who will execute its particulars; indeed, sometimes even a wrong idea can benefit from sensitive vetting, as there may be a motivation behind it that proves to be of immeasurable value once it has been teased forth. There is the moment, too, when one's initial vision becomes the joint property of the entire creative team, and that is especially satisfying: everyone works harder, grows more enthusiastic, brings ever more to the table, and becomes more open to others' contributions. It is wonderful—a gift—to be able to sit before a blank page with a pencil and to begin. But a house is meant for living, and nothing can fill that house with life quite so richly—so lastingly—as the spirit of collaboration.

It is a cliché to say so, but I find it to be true: an architect, especially a practitioner specializing in residences, is only as good as his clients, and over the course of some 1,200 projects I have been especially blessed in this regard. One of the largest, least spoken about challenges in my profession involves the earning of people's faith. This is entirely understandable. Any creative endeavor is to a greater or lesser extent a voyage into the unknown; there are no guarantees. My clients can express their aspirations with eloquence and show me pictures, I can present plans and elevations and construct models, but they still have to keep the faith that what they are describing—the hazy fantasies in their minds—will transform, in my hands, into reality. Yet it is that effort of faith-building and education—really a two-way street, for I must trust and learn as well—that ultimately allows me to be more creative, and my clients to get more from their projects than might otherwise have been the case.

Another thing I admire about John Singer Sargent: he knew when to stop, one of the hardest calculations for any artist. I think now is the time. Let the journey begin.

I.
RESPECT FOR TRADITION

I am as proud of my accomplishments as the next architect, and over the course of my decades in practice, I have done my share of boasting. But I'd be a foolish man indeed if I failed to acknowledge that there is, truly, nothing new under the sun. Everything has been done, and done better than I could ever possibly do it. And so learning from the past remains essential to design as I practice it.

Nevertheless, it is our instinct as human beings to absorb all of the best ideas around us and combine them in novel ways. One of the great examples of this, in our time, is the iPhone. Seemingly so original, this communication device is actually a compendium of preexisting technologies—some of them, such as GPS, decades old. What is visionary is the way in which these technologies have been altered, updated, and combined. If in fact there are no new ideas, there *are* new ways of adapting and applying the old ones, and that is what I attempt to achieve in the creation of traditional projects.

There are multiple examples of this kind of thinking in my own homes. The entrance to my stone tower is a Roman arch, a means of spanning space that, as the name implies, is a product of antiquity. The arch remains as simple, beautiful, and useful as it was when Caesar strode beneath one, and though I'd like to claim credit for its invention, that accolade belongs to an architect who did his drafting in a toga. I can, however, claim credit for combining a traditional stone Roman arch with industrial-style steel-and-glass doors to create an entrance to the tower that interleaves history and modernity. Let me add that I have not chosen to do so for novelty's sake, nor to show off the depth of my learning. Rather, I have adapted the arch out of respect for all that it represents: a timeless, eloquent beauty that derives from proportion, materiality, tectonics, engineering, and problem-solving. I have adapted it, in short, out of a respect for tradition.

This impulse toward adaptation is bound up tightly with a sense of place, and, if I may say so, no region expresses this more vividly, or with greater imagination, than the American South. One of the great things about classicism is that it travels well through both space and time—from pharaonic Cairo to the modern Georgia town of the same name—and the antebellum mansions that still stand as icons in the landscape combine the language of Robert Adam with the physical reality of a place where the temperature feels equatorial, stone was unavailable, and skilled labor proved to be in short supply. Yet those nineteenth-century French and English architects—sweating in their hats and suits, often representing Northern clients but intrigued by the potential of heart pine and virgin-growth cypress—braided the local vernacular with the classical tradition in a way that, to my eye, has seldom been equaled. Classicism for its own sake has never inspired me. I am mostly concerned with the *experience* of architecture—which is to say, how it feels. Few things feel as real and comfortable—as *right*—as the historic classicism of the South.

I have a great and abiding love of, and respect for, tradition—and one of the great traditions of the architecture of my region is a willingness to experiment, to honor the past but to break out of it. One thing my predecessors knew for certain: the piano has many keys. Why be limited?

ATLANTA CLASSICISM

This house, in Atlanta's Buckhead district, has a good deal of history embedded in it—architectural and local history and, as a matter of fact, my own. Constructed in 1922, the residence was designed by Neel Reid, whose firm, Hentz, Reid & Adler, created many of Atlanta's—indeed, the region's—finest buildings. For the distinctive, stately front facade, Reid elegantly adapted the *rear* elevation of Tintinhull House in Somerset, England, which is famous for its Arts and Crafts–style garden. The great Georgia classicist did a superlative job, and I can say that with not a little authority: I lived right across the street from the house for twenty years and passed many hours contemplating not only the architecture itself, but also the ways in which it captures the light, from dawn till sunset, in every season. I was proud and pleased to be asked to give this contribution to Atlanta's architectural and social history contemporary relevance.

That famous front, and the side facades to a depth of about thirty feet, remained intact. Beyond that, I took off the back of the house and replaced it with a new volume enclosing a master suite and sitting room above and a family room and screen porch below. We also gutted the remaining interior space, rearranging the plan and making the rooms more commodious, and shaped a half-dome from former attic space to bring light into the house's center via the oculus window in the gable.

The design also benefited from my close proximity. Over the years, the previous owner's landscapers had mounded up the soil in the front of the house until it covered part of the entry stairs, which (being a fastidious sort) had begun to drive me a bit crazy. When my services were engaged, the first thing I did was grab a shovel, cross the street, and start digging. My excavations revealed that the front step took the form of a volute, the scrollwork element typically integrated into an Ionic capital. For a moment I imagined myself a modern-day Filippo Brunelleschi, picking through the ruins of my own personal Rome. I carried my discovery not only to the new back stairs on the garden facade, but into the house, where I placed a volute on the bottom of the relocated front stairway.

PREVIOUS SPREAD: The front facade, constructed from Indiana limestone, is modeled after the rear elevation of Tintinhull House, in Somerset, England, which dates from the seventeenth century. OPPOSITE: A pair of stone eagles flank the entrance to the motor court and give the house its name.

For the new garden facade, I challenged myself to mine history as imaginatively as Neel Reid had done in front. My design drew on the exquisite colonnade of the Erechtheum, the fifth-century B.C. temple on the Acropolis; the eighteenth-century Scottish architect Robert Adam's elegant liberty-taking with the classical orders; and the Mannerist tradition, whose influence can be felt in the way the outer columns morph into the low wall on the terrace. Regarding this last idea, I was inspired by the realization that the lower third of a column is very nearly straight, and therefore it made sense to combine the wall and shaft into a single element, above which the entasis begins. The sculptural gesture is an intellectual and creative solution to a centuries-old problem and explains my love of classicism: rather than being a rigid style, it remains endlessly supple and open to interpretation. A lot of contemporary classicism, I have observed, resists playing more than one note. But to extract the vernacular—or, indeed, the modern—is to violate the style's welcoming spirit. That is knowledge that Mnesicles, likely the architect of the Erechtheum, held as surely as did Neel Reid, and I am happy to inherit it.

The garden was a collaboration between myself and the landscape architect John Howard, who had been tasked by the owners with creating a plan that approximated what Reid might have done. This was complicated by the fact that much of the once-capacious property had been sold off over the years, and achieving a balance between an elegant parterre in the old style and useful open space proved tricky. Eventually we developed an effective compromise: a flat tableau of grass with corners comprised of clipped hedges and flowering schemes. In the course of excavating the property, I also made the rather startling discovery that the original driveway had been nearly five feet lower and was filled in as part of an effort to raise the backyard. John and I worked together to return the drive to where it had been, gracefully opening the way to under-the-house parking and additional garden space via the removal of the garage.

I loved working on this project. It was the fourth house I'd designed for this particular client, whom I liked and knew well, and who gave me the latitude to get it right. And, of course, as my garden elevation is really the sort you'd find on the front of a house, you might say that I took Tintinhull and flipped it around again.

I reconfigured the plan, removing some walls and all of the interior finishes.
This was formerly the back stair; I increased the foyer space and moved
the stair to the front, incorporating a volute—a key component in the design
of the original exterior stair—into the landing at the turn in the banister.

In the original living room, the walls featured applied architectural details. I redesigned the panel profiles and configurations—all of which are made of hand-carved wood—to be more proportionate to the newly enlarged space.

ABOVE: We carried the leaded-glass motif from the house's windows into the interior cabinetry in the butler's pantry. A space that previously did not exist, it bridges the old and new parts of the residence. OPPOSITE: The dining room was an existing space to which we added a more elaborate and refined crown molding.

RIGHT: The kitchen sits in the house's new addition; because it communicates with the family room, we increased its domestic character by eliminating upper cabinets and adding curtains in sympathy with its companion space. OVERLEAF, LEFT AND RIGHT: John Howard's garden design reflects the historic original while bringing the home into the present day. The gate, with its Lutyens-esque stair, opens onto a turning court for guest parking.

RIGHT: The Indiana limestone garden facade features volutes at the foot of the stairs that morph into the fountain's border; similarly, the portico's outermost columns seem to grow out of the terrace walls.

OVERLEAF: A screen porch was added to the house's southern facade and extends the family room. The medallion over the fireplace came from the family's collection of objects.

AN ORIGINAL PATH

When you walk the woods, you discover pathways created by those who've preceded you. Most of these trails were forged by animals, others by two-legged creatures. Either way, what you notice, if you choose to follow them, is how naturally these routes carry you to your destination. This is because they have evolved from instinct—an intuitive feel for how best to navigate the terrain—rather than having a design imposed upon the land that is at odds with the way it wants to be used. Though this approach to a site may seem better suited to natural conditions, I have found it invaluable in deciding where, and how, to place a building on a property and even the best way to develop an architectural plan. If one can let go of one's preconceptions and open oneself to the immutable character of a site, one will often end up with a house that flows more naturally and inevitably, as opposed to a structure that has been twisted into something that was never meant to be.

Consider this house. It sits on an uneven parcel that tumbles down to the Long Island Sound in a somewhat exclusive New England town that is an enclave of tradition and prosperity. At a glance, the building appears rather formal. It's a Norman-style house with a steeply pitched roof that reflects the preferences of the owners, for whom I designed a home in a similar style down South—call it the 2.0 version of their primary residence. Yet the house is not entirely as it seems. My clients aren't formal people and pursue their interests in fine art and gee-whiz gadgetry with equal enthusiasm. Accordingly, their home reflects their character, which relies as much on instinct and emotion as logic—and thus has more in common with a "naturally designed" landscape than it does with its buttoned-up, stately neighbors.

Here I must confess that I didn't plan to take this approach. Ordinarily, when I design a house of this scale, I follow a pattern that reflects a codified program: you park your car here, you bring your groceries in there, that element transitions into the kitchen, and so forth. This doesn't represent a cookie-cutter methodology; it is, rather, the way the big-house typology works. But when I

OPPOSITE: A view from the library into the front-entry foyer. Painted wood paneling surrounds the doorway. OVERLEAF: The house sits at the highest elevation on its site overlooking the Long Island Sound; the lower wing encloses the pool. Both volumes employ large areas of view-friendly expressed glass.

The living room features a cove ceiling, a nod to my clients'
previous home in Atlanta, on which we also collaborated.
Both actually and psychologically, the high windows piercing
the thick walls convey a sense of protection and permanence.
They also project illumination into the tall space.

traveled up north to begin design development, I happened to stay in a hotel room in which the coffee machine was next to the bed. That arrangement offered a degree of convenience I thoroughly enjoyed, even though it would never occur to me to do the same thing at home. This led me to think about travel, how it opens you to different ways of living and makes you amenable to new kinds of thinking. Thus primed, when I arrived at the site and considered the terrain, I realized that the natural place to site the garage was not behind the house but beside it, and that the confluence of the two would be the living room. *That* meant that rather than following the usual route—from garage to mudroom to kitchen—the residents would enter the foyer and proceed through the living room to the kitchen.

That simple reconsideration of the way things are usually done, based on an openness to the site and how it might be most naturally occupied, changed everything. It meant that the space that's usually out of sight, out of mind—the formal living room—could be absorbed into the day-to-day life of the house and thus enjoyed and appreciated, based on nothing more than the flow of the plan. It also enabled me to bring the main stair, which connects the public rooms to the second- and third-floor bedrooms, down to the same dynamic connection point in the foyer.

This approach may seem unconventional, but in fact it pulled the design together in a way that was more impactful, enabled my clients to use more of their house (and to use it naturally), and also responded comprehensively to the ways in which the different members of the household really live. Thus what began with a coffee machine in a hotel room evolved into an effective design for living.

If on the main floor the plan responded to the site, on the second level we chose consciously to continue the lesson and tailor the design to my clients' predilections, as opposed to domestic convention. This is most evident in the couple's private quarters, which are entered via the room-size master closet. In all my years of practice, I've never designed a house in which you walked through a closet to get to a bedroom. It was my clients' idea, and quite a practical one, given how much the husband travels, how often his days begin and end at the packing station. The residents obeyed their hearts, and the result is effective functionally and aesthetically.

OPPOSITE: A vignette in the living room features a tall Miró and a diminutive Picasso. The interior design was created by my frequent collaborator Beth Webb.

RIGHT: The family room, a counterpoint to the library on the opposite side of the house, communicates directly with the kitchen and overlooks the lawn and, beyond it, the Long Island Sound. The reclaimed-oak beams are part of the tectonic language of strong, elegantly chiseled wood that extends throughout the residence.

OVERLEAF: Jeremy Smearman developed the landscape design, which at once enfolds the house and embraces its surroundings.

The design's open embrace of function and condition also produced another unexpected benefit: there is no house behind the house. Whereas in more traditional layouts, one finds the living and dining rooms in front and the kitchen and family room in the rear, the plan is such that there are axial views through all of the main floor's spaces and, indeed, cross-axial sight lines to the landscape and water. The plan makes what is undeniably a large house feel more graspable and welcoming, and the link to the out-of-doors produces the warmth and comfort that only an easy connection to the natural environment can provide. This formulation works vertically as well: moving up and down the stair, with its capacious landings and expansive glazing, one experiences a prismatic scenography of interior and exterior tableaux, at once sweeping and intimate.

The interior designer, Beth Webb, achieved an outcome that was no less adroit. Our mutual clients brought to their new home a remarkably eclectic mix of modern and traditional (bordering on medieval) furniture, as well as artworks equally separated by time and genre—all of which arrived from the residents' previous, and much smaller, home. Somehow Beth was able to bring these radically different elements into balance with one another with sensitivity and grace, and to fill in the spaces between them with components that suited the scale of the old furniture and the new architecture. The house feels both comfortable and cohesive, and it required a talent as subtle as Beth's to achieve it.

When I consider the house, which has proven so well tailored to the desires of my clients (individually and as a family), I am reminded that it is not as unconventional as it seems, because the modern mind isn't always linear. We've become used to going online and following our noses from site to site, link to link, obeying no greater logic than our own curiosities and instincts; this organic transit feels far more natural than the straight-ahead one we might follow if the rules of cyber-engagement were more conventional. Perhaps the Internet has led us back to what the creature in the woods seems always to have known: that the lack of expectation of a linear path predisposes us to doing what makes sense. There is no firmer expression of that idea, in my work, than this house.

OPPOSITE: In the kitchen, the reclaimed oak used in the expansive handcrafted island, an object of my design, is a match for both the beams in the adjoining family room and the wide-plank floor.

Adjacent to the family room and the kitchen, the dining room also overlooks the indoor pool from an interior window at right, above the banquette. Beyond the tall French windows lies a terrace with a water view.

The library is identical in scale to the family room, which occupies a mirror-image position on the opposite side of the living room. With natural light on two sides, the room balances an enfolding interiority with a connection to the landscape. OVERLEAF: The pool captures reflections from the garden beyond the bronze reclining nude.

A CHANGE OF PLAN

This project, for which we combined three lots on a cul-de-sac that abutted a golf course, demonstrates how one can liberate a house from traditional expectations and constraints—even when it's designed and constructed in a traditional style.

What makes this place a bit of a traitor to its class is the plan. When I sat down to draw it, I invented a narrative in which a historic residence, with an entry court flanked by a pair of horse barns, was updated, so that one of the barns became a garage and the other was a grand master suite with sleeping, bathing, and dressing areas. I was, of course, designing a brand-new, ground-up house. But applying this bit of speculative fiction enabled me to extract a large component of the program—specifically, the main sleeping quarters—from the house's primary volume. This facilitated an unusual move: the creation of a floor plan that neatly combined traditional and contemporary rooms without violating the clean volumetric character of the box.

When you enter the foyer, you can go left, into the formal, compartmentalized library and living room, or right, into the relaxed, freely intercommunicating family room and kitchen. The foyer bridges these zones in front; on the garden elevation, they are connected by the rather grand dining room. The stair, which lies at the core, leads up to a second floor with four secondary bed-and-bath suites—one in each corner. The plan is simple, logical, legible, and axial; the master suite, residing in its own wing, enjoys absolute privacy, and the entirety, despite its in-built unconventionality, still represents a reassuringly traditional manor.

I also streamlined the structure's aesthetic character. It is meant to be a classic northern French château, studiously stripped of the style cues typically applied to French country houses. Outwardly, this house remains as clean and volumetric as I could make it—and therefore more modern, despite its vernacular antecedents.

In a similar vein, the interiors rely on scale, material, and craft, rather than ornament, to achieve their effect, and in this regard I was abetted by a longtime collaborator, the interior designer Barbara Westbrook. I set the architectural direction and handled crafting and adjusting the frame, while Barbara selected the woods and finishes, chose colors, and designed the kitchen and pantry spaces. I appreciate Barbara's style, which I find to be at once sophisticated and contemporary—and her attraction to symmetry has found its way into my own thinking. As well, I appreciate Barbara's sense of decorum and commitment to such traditional components as formal dining rooms. These are qualities I tend to ascribe to the South. But they travel quite well and widely—even as far as the Loire.

OPPOSITE: Black Belgian limestone paves the floor of the house's foyer. Windows and doors imported from France are a key feature of the overall design: their texture and craft contrast with the simple, sculptural plaster walls. OVERLEAF: The entry court is flanked by two projecting wings, one of which contains the master suite, the other the garage.

In the living room, the gentle transition from walls to ceiling makes the room feel taller—with the crisp line of a crown molding absent, nothing stops the eye as it drifts upward. The portal at right leads to the library; straight ahead is the dining room.

OPPOSITE AND ABOVE: The interior designer Barbara Westbrook's choice of
a deep chocolate color for the dining room walls at once makes the space
feel rich and intimate and stimulates the appetite. The room is cozy at night
and receives abundant natural light from the adjoining back porch by day.

Barbara Westbrook designed the kitchen island, which is painted the color of an aircraft carrier and feels nearly as big; the bent "legs" at the corners add an entertainingly surreal touch. The side cabinets are constructed from oak; the beams impart an agreeably rustic "country kitchen" character to the room.

The kitchen communicates directly with the family room, which is flooded with sunlight from windows on three sides. Barbara Westbrook's design conveys a particularly Southern combination of propriety and ease, and her color palette complements the overall sunniness.

An upstairs guest room also eliminates the crease between walls and ceiling, which I find has a softening effect desirable in bedrooms. The temporal quality in a curvaceous room is especially appealing, as the light moves by increments rather than abruptly. The hand-troweled unpainted plaster walls display their texture and a slightly mottled color palette. OVERLEAF, LEFT AND RIGHT: The oculus above the tub in the master bath brings in light while maintaining privacy. I used the same marble on the counter and tub-surround surfaces and floor, in tiles for the latter.

The simple, rational plan of the house resulted in an experience of surpassing serenity and elegance.

OPPOSITE: On the back porch, the ceiling boards are wood, the floor is limestone, and the walls are made of lime washed brick—a combination of textures that forms a strong bond with the garden.

ENGLISH INFLUENCE

The term *McMansion*, which denotes a steroidal architectural pile that pulls together a grab bag of typically classical references into a gigantic aesthetic train wreck, has become somewhat overused in recent years. But the fact remains that for a long time, the moment an American made big money, he or she went out and built something that made Tara look like a toolshed. So it is with not a little pleasure that I can report a bend in the road of this trend: many folks who previously resided in 15,000-square-foot homes are deciding it is time to downsize—in this case, from a large home to a new 4,000-square-foot cottage.

The challenge was less architectural and more territorial. My clients had purchased a sizable corner property—very nearly an acre—in Atlanta's Buckhead district, on a street so famous for its grand manor houses (historic and contemporary) that it's regularly traversed by tour buses. So while this couple wanted to embrace a simpler life, they'd chosen to do it on a property that, rather than affording privacy and discretion, potentially placed them on display.

The thrust of the architecture we discovered with relative ease: the couple expressed a love of the early-twentieth-century English cottage style with an Arts and Crafts influence, and I—having recently returned from a visit to the Cotswolds, where I'd made a close, pleasurable study of this particular genre—was very happy to oblige. The outcome was a simple one-story house with the bedrooms tucked into the roof, its materials and decoration influenced by the great masters of the form, Charles Voysey and Edwin Lutyens. The place proved modest in scale but not materiality: the flat clay roof tiles were created by Ludowici, a historic manufacturer located in Ohio, and the creamy limestone from which the walls were constructed came from a quarry in Fond du Lac, Wisconsin. Though the rooms themselves aren't grand—the study measures eleven by fifteen feet—the ceilings surprise with their height, and I introduced a palette of details, including moldings and paneling, that draw on the richly worked Arts and Crafts vocabulary.

OPPOSITE: Throughout the house, I used pieces of broken roof tile to create vividly expressed exterior detailing. OVERLEAF: The brick driveway, clay-tile roof, and limestone exterior immediately establish the language of this residence.

My greatest pleasure on this project involved the exterior detailing, for which I used damaged flat clay tiles in a decorative manner on headers, above doors and windows, and around columns. This involved trimming the broken tiles with a masonry saw and cementing them to expose their narrow thin edges, which are marked with lines that resemble the kind of hatch marks you might produce while you're doodling. This added a certain rustic vitality to the design and also created a sense of narrative by suggesting that the arches and keystones I created had filled in larger openings left over from an earlier incarnation of the house.

But shaping the property itself remained the project's Everest, one I climbed with my longtime collaborator, the landscape architect Jeremy Smearman. After much contemplation, Jeremy resolved the privacy issue by lowering the building site very slightly, so that it was on grade with the corner lot's side street and slightly below the level of the more heavily trafficked boulevard in front; he then constructed a wall that hid the curving entry drive from view. This Jeremy complemented with a charming English-style garden on the house's other side, using plant material to create privacy from the side street. It's a corner lot on one of the busiest thoroughfares in Buckhead, but thanks to Jeremy's ministrations the cottage feels snugly nestled into its surroundings, an utterly peaceful retreat.

Though this is the first such residence that I've completed, I look forward to doing more "ensmalling" in the future—creating well-designed modest houses that deliver, with elegance and discernment, no more than just what you need.

OPPOSITE: The entry porch and front door feature
Arts and Crafts–style paneling and detail.

Though the house is comparatively small, certain rooms are surprisingly voluminous. The living room reveals painted wood beams and continues the architectural language of the English cottage style in the paneling and details.

PREVIOUS SPREAD, LEFT: My organic design for the gate abstracts the idea of developing flowers and grasses. PREVIOUS SPREAD, RIGHT: The applied arch, with the window below it, contributes to the architectural narrative by suggesting that at some point the entire opening was larger. RIGHT: Jeremy Smearman's garden design sets an intimate outdoor room within a larger pastoral setting.

II.
RUSTIC RETREATS

One of the most precious commodities in contemporary life, I think we would all agree, is peace. It is the reason people purchase large tracts of land. To experience the myriad natural sounds that collectively comprise a perfect silence. To know a darkness unbroken by the light of subdivisions. To commune with no one other than the person within. The price of peace, of course, is eternal vigilance, as everyone you know wants to borrow it from you. But once achieved, there can be no greater satisfaction.

And it is from that perfect peace that the rustic pleasures arise, differing from season to season. In the hot months, I like to bushhog late in the day, when the sun is low and the promise of cooler temperatures draws me off the porch. After an hour on the tractor with the heat and dust and vibration, with the chaff flying and the rabbits darting out from under, I enter the lower field when the sun is almost setting, and the sudden coolness, the fog settling in swirling layers, envelops like a shock to the senses. In winter, I'll walk the frozen furrows peppered with animal footprints, breathing the kind of cold that cracks the lungs. The smell of woodsmoke, the dry rustle of cornstalks, testify to the depths of the season in the South.

What I am describing, to be sure, is experiential. If it speaks to your soul, all you really require to achieve it is a sweet parcel of land and some shelter. Yet, if properly executed, architecture can heighten the experience, and that is my objective for the rustic retreats I am called upon to create: having become intimate, and empathetic, with my own surroundings, I can draw on a wellspring of peace and put it within reach of others.

For me, no surprise, it all begins with the land. Typically, a client will already have a strong emotional connection to the ground he or she has purchased, and so our first get-together is usually on-site, where we walk the property and consider the opportunities presented by the topography, the sun and wind, the vistas, and the flora. Because a rural retreat is often a second home, where ease of life and taking in the views are large considerations, this conversation provides the seed that gives form to the house.

I am fortunate to have grown up with a father who taught college-level botany (as an artist, my dad also possesses a subtle, superlative hand, of which I am intermittently envious), so it is easy for me to speak the language of landscape architecture and grasp the basic principles. But siting is the genesis for so many of the ideas that go into a house, and so I always collaborate with a professional: it allows for the expansion of my ideas into new, entirely unanticipated realms. At some point, I will step away and allow the work to continue without interference. But if we start off in the same direction, it builds a momentum that finds its way into all aspects of the project.

As with other of life's pleasures, of course, too much rusticity can be troublesome. In the South, our response to this conundrum is the porch. I won't say we invented it, but I am sure we perfected it. The porch represents the middle zone between the conditioned and the uncovered and permits us the exquisite pleasure of keeping one foot in comfort and the other in the wild. As porches increasingly become as heavily accessorized, and as expensive, as family rooms—tricked out with fireplaces, kitchenettes, pizza ovens, sofas upholstered in weatherproof chintz, and flat-screen TVs—the pendulum might be swinging too far in the direction of civilization. Yet lest you think that humankind has gone fatally soft, let me note that defining *the verge*—the line we are compelled to draw between the designed and the haphazard, the interior and the out-of-doors—is an impulse common to all creatures and, indeed, an essential component of the natural condition.

At my home in the country, I maintain an expanse of well-barbered green that extends for a distance beyond the porch, enclosed by a low stone wall that separates it from the untended land beyond. One of my great porch-sitting activities involves watching quail jump up on that wall from the fields and think about what they propose to do. When they're feeling adventurous, they take the plunge and dash crazily across my lawn. And when whatever constitutes nerve in a quail fails them, the birds fall back into the familiar safety of the weeds. Watching this drama has taught me that all living creatures are drawn to the verge—the point of demarcation between the well-kept and the wild—and the choice between going forward and holding back creates energy, interest, and a palpable sense of the presence of life itself. Rusticity is a great and enduring gift. But contrasting it with a manicured condition makes both more powerful than either would be on its own.

I will also, as house and landscape move forward together, engage my clients in a process of education—about the land itself, its history and legacy, and also regarding the idea of stewardship. Learning about the latter helps them to appreciate what it is they're undertaking— to be responsible toward the property and, in time, leave it better than they found it. As Mark Twain said, "Buy land, they're not making it anymore." And though Twain probably didn't mean it this way, ownership of your own special patch of the planet implies an investment in the future in every way.

MODERN PASTORAL

For those who might be seeking a reliable definition of heaven on earth, you'd do well to consider Blackberry Farm. Situated on 4,200 pristine acres in the foothills of Tennessee's Great Smoky Mountains, the hotel and resort is known for its farm-to-table cuisine and comprehensive wine cellar, both of which can be enjoyed in one of the most restorative, arcadian settings to be found anywhere in America. Several years ago, Blackberry began to offer opportunities for private ownership, and I designed the first of several getaway homes there. I found it to be an exceptional opportunity—not least for my collaboration with one of the farm's founding visionaries, Kreis Beall, whose rich understanding of rural building typologies and personal generosity and enthusiasm had a lasting impact on my work. At Blackberry, I was also able to apply my thinking to what amounts to a still-evolving form: the new Southern second home.

There could be no more fertile design laboratory. First and foremost, because it is a farm, elements like reclaimed materials, hand-hewn logs, and barn board are important design components and contribute strongly to establishing a sense of place. As the houses are being constructed in a resort where many meals are prepared by Blackberry's gourmet chefs and then delivered, I can think very freely about the kitchens: with major culinary operations outsourced, their floor plans can be less formal and more closely associated with porch or terrace. One of the most transformative influences, interestingly enough, is the fact that golf carts are the primary mode of transportation—which means there's no need for an attached garage. This element typically constitutes the largest room in a house, and thus ends up owning the largest part of the roof. Not having that as my primary architectural driver (so to speak) means that I can design residences with the clean, simple proportions that existed back when there was a carriage barn at a remove from the main house.

OPPOSITE: Reclaimed barn siding, laid up like shiplap, encloses an artfully disguised garage at this Blackberry Farm vacation residence.

RIGHT: The house's foyer features an opening into the kitchen at left and steps leading up to a master suite on the right. My architectural narrative conceived of the suite as a cottage that had been constructed at another level on the sloping property and the house itself as a separate building—perhaps a converted barn—with a structure featuring contemporary glass doors and a vaulted ceiling crafted to unite the two. OVERLEAF: The kitchen opens onto the dining area and, beyond it, the living room. The ubiquity of the painted wood planks adds to the narrative of an older structure that was updated without losing its essential character.

ABOVE: The snug master bedroom, where the watchwords were ease, comfort, and coziness. All of the interiors were designed by Kreis Beall, Blackberry Farm's presiding aesthetic visionary. OPPOSITE: A copper cylinder in the style of a Japanese soaking tub features a small stair to facilitate entry.

The pavilion-like stone entry with a lively stone gable sits between the bedroom cottage at right and the main house. The picturesque character of the architecture suggests an assemblage that found its shape over time.

The homes I've executed thus far make for an interesting collision of materials and forms. I have given a modern twist to the traditional, warm reclaimed-wood siding—considered the most "authentic" part of each project—by mounting it vertically and pairing it with more contemporary glass-and-steel windows and doors for greater transparency and connection to the land; though the shape of each structure is recognizably that of a vernacular farm building, the renderings are modernist and reductive, with the moldings, overhangs, and rakes removed to reveal the pure form of the house. Thus the picture that emerges at Blackberry expresses the reality of modern life: brief vacations of a few days to a week, in a clean, compact, approachably scaled residence.

As for the plans, they reflect the fact that, at Blackberry, there really is no distinction between front of house and back, formal or informal; rather, rooms are arranged side by side and connected not by hallways, but by axial paths that eliminate hierarchies of space and strengthen the relationship to the land. Farm buildings are sheds rather than neoclassical residences, and my work at Blackberry reflects the distinction.

One of the most appealing aspects of our efforts in this paradise involves my preferred gambit for down-massing the houses: breaking them up into miniature compounds, small suites of structures that separate the program into discrete components. This enables me to create separate guest quarters, a car barn (if one is required), even a stand-alone library or study. The so-called "big house" can be little more than a kitchen with an attached porch.

If there is a presiding idea driving my interpretation of the new Southern second home, it is a simple one: that of freedom. Freedom from overbearing mass and complex function, freedom from the affectations of everyday life, and consequently the freedom to enjoy light, space, nature, and, most of all, peace. The life of a farmer is labor-intensive, but life on a farm is life at its essence and beautifully, ineffably sweet. That's what I seek to achieve at Blackberry.

OPPOSITE: Like the siding on pages 102-103, the reclaimed siding on this guest cottage is laid up vertically to give a modern twist to a vernacular idea. The lower window belongs to a kitchenette; the one above, in the gable, illuminates the sleeping loft. OVERLEAF: The study in the main house (right) overlooks the guest accommodations (left), providing a suitably appealing visual object.

PAGES 102–103 Laying up the siding vertically on the doors and gable makes this classic vernacular building more contemporary and, indeed, more abstract. PREVIOUS SPREAD, LEFT AND RIGHT: At another project I completed at Blackberry Farm, a living/dining porch features a slender iron rail atop the wooden one, which brings it up to code height without obscuring the sight lines. RIGHT: At the same house, the stone walls seem to grow out of the guest cottage.

RIGHT: The gabled end is finished in a dry-stacked local stone. As with the vertical barn siding, the monolithic application of the material gives the house a more contemporary character within a traditional context. OVERLEAF: The colors on the porch swing fabrics nicely abstract the American flag.

HIGH-COUNTRY RETREAT

There is something about possessing a great abundance of land, on our increasingly populous planet, that does indeed seem like the ultimate luxury. The people for whom I designed this lodge, in the North Carolina high country, held in their hands just such a blessing: more than one hundred acres, some of it commanding a mountaintop, and with a "borrowed" landscape that includes tens of thousands of acres of protected parkland. My clients wanted to build a large family home, a place where they could spend considerable time and not use only as a weekend retreat. They knew what they had, and they were humbled by it. Frankly, so was I. The great naturalist Aldo Leopold once asked, "Of what avail are forty freedoms without a blank spot on the map?" We were about to occupy one of those precious blank spots, and with a structure that would make its presence known. I felt more than my usual sense of duty, not just to my clients, but to the circumstances, to get it right.

I enlisted the landscape architect Jeremy Smearman, who has a special ability to see the micro and macro of a setting, to help me determine how best to integrate the house and everything that supported it. As much finesse went into shaping the half-mile-long road that forms the approach as the building site; Jeremy used boulders, retaining walls, and a certain amount of clearing to create a drive that was effective, both infrastructurally and aesthetically, then "healed the wounds" we'd inflicted with new plantings that will, over time, restore the setting to a semblance of virgin ground.

The two-acre building site demanded the same kind of attention—only more so. The place Jeremy and I selected with the clients was actually on a mountaintop, but that didn't mean it was level. The property needed to be graded in such a way that I had flat land on which to build, but with subtle shifts, so as to suggest the natural movement of the earth; despite the abundance of forest, we had to bring in a number of mature trees and get them settled in the thin soil so that the long, linear house I had drawn would feel naturally, comfortably nestled.

PREVIOUS SPREAD: The extraordinary panorama offered by the North Carolina high country made this sitting area essential. OPPOSITE: Beyond the porte-cochere is the house's motor court and guest wing. The long winding drive was developed by landscape architect Jeremy Smearman. I used the roofing slates as siding on the upper story.

The two-story, one-room-thick house, nearly ten thousand square feet in size, which stretches across the property so that its public and private components can participate equally in the views, conveys a number of influences. It possesses an English DNA but remains strongly rooted in the materials of North Carolina; additionally, a house of this scale and style, partaking of such a setting, must inevitably owe something to "parkitecture," as the design language of the great lodges of the National Park Service has been called. To cite an example, if you look beneath the slate-clad back dormers (very English in character), you'll see simple wood haunches holding up the overhang, an unmistakable touch of the frontier. It's the vicarage meets the bunkhouse—to my mind, an appealing bricolage of elements.

A word I believe applies to this residence—though one that might not readily come to anyone else's mind—is *minimalist*. Inside and out, the architectural gestures and components are relatively few and held in restraint, which I believe underlies the great sense of peace the place conveys. In this regard, my twenty-two-year collaboration with Jeremy was critical as well. He and I have spoken at length about the idea of selecting better and fewer trees and placing them for maximum impact, rather than bringing in a large number and scattering them in an ad hoc plan. The right material, the appropriate idea, the culminating placement—these are applicable equally to architecture and landscape and, when braided seamlessly, mean everything to the particular success of this house.

PREVIOUS SPREAD: The house's main facade, constructed from local granite and Indiana limestone. To site the house, the mountaintop had to be cleared and regraded, after which new trees and plantings were introduced. OPPOSITE: The carved limestone entrance sitting between the two stone gables looks a bit like the entrance to a university building in Cambridge (England, not Massachusetts), right down to the flanking bollards. OVERLEAF: The entry is deep enough to accommodate a pair of niches filled with planted urns. The thumb-latch hardware on the front door is contrastingly informal and ties the architecture back to the region.

PREVIOUS SPREAD, LEFT AND
RIGHT: A view through the foyer
into the library from the stairwell.
All of the woodwork, floors
included, is crafted from local
white oak. RIGHT: The lodge-like
living room, which measures
twenty-four by thirty-eight
feet, overlooks the back terrace
and the house's major view.

Both indoors and out, the challenge
of this house was to combine
authority and humility, and never
to overshadow the land.

OPPOSITE: Dormered light scoops fill the upper reaches of the living
room with natural illumination. The notion of keeping the lower reaches
of the major rooms clad in stained oak in order to draw the eye
upward to lighter plasterwork ceilings arrived early in the design process.
Nashville woodworker James Dunn crafted the paneling.

The screen porch, accessed via the doors flanking the fireplace in the living room, is notably less formal and more embracing of the out-of-doors. The walls are finished in board-and-batten siding, and the beams and woodwork white-painted.

ABOVE: On the one hand the Gothic console table suits the "Mr. Chips" aspect of the house's character, while on the other its simple finish is entirely appropriate to the rural surroundings. OPPOSITE: The screen porch features a seating area off of the outdoor fireplace, as well as a dining zone. OVERLEAF: Behind the house, Jeremy Smearman created vantage points from which to enjoy the view.

SOUTHERN SIMPLICITY

There are certain art forms, for example painting or writing, in which the lag time between conception and execution is near to zero. You have the idea, instinct, or inspiration and, with a flourish of the brush or the stroke of a pen, it is accomplished. This telescoping of time can take place in architecture, and I am happy to say that, in my life, it has usually been thus. In the case of this particular house, however, a four-bedroom Italianate villa in Knoxville, Tennessee, there was a space of six years between design and construction. In *The Glass Menagerie*, Tennessee Williams observes that "time is the longest distance between two places," and that certainly was the case with this project—in fact, it was a distance long enough for me to become a different sort of creative spirit. The long-delayed construction of the house afforded the chance to revisit, vividly, the younger architect I once had been—and to discover that the child still had much to teach the man.

For an ostensibly urban property, the site was quite big, nearly seven acres, and blessed with not only an intriguing topography, but also beautiful light. When the owners found me, I was just finishing up a Santa Fe–inspired project and remained very much absorbed in the building styles of the Southwest: the emphasis on mass and volume, the thick walls and simple gestures, and the way the strong, clear desert sun affected those components.

In this respect, I proved to be in sympathy with my clients, a couple with refined, discerning tastes and a great attraction to simplicity. As the house took shape, they would study my drawings and ask, diplomatically, "Can't we do less?" This struck me at first as somewhat odd, as I am by inclination a minimalist. But the design, I realized, remained quite rich in detail—moldings, trims, mantelpieces—because that's what architects do. As my clients encouraged me to reduce, my mind drifted back to the desert, to the adobe structures devoid of almost everything but form, and I began to conflate the Santa Fe style with the Italianate villa on my drawing board.

PREVIOUS SPREAD: The house's arrival court has three entry doors, all of which open into the foyer; the windows above belong to a pair of guest rooms. John Howard served as the landscape architect. OPPOSITE: On the back of the house, a covered porch with overscaled Doric columns, Etruscan in inspiration, is expressive and bold.

138

And because the sun on the site was so significant—the landscape transforming steadily and by exquisite degrees with its passage—I began to think as well of the painter Joseph Mallard William Turner and his singular ability to represent form as light. That, I decided, was what I wanted to do: eliminate the details, purify the forms, and make the project about illumination.

With the enthusiasm of youth, I began to experiment, finding ways to draw in the sun on three sides of a room, eliminating the upper kitchen cabinets to open up views, curving ceilings and softening the edges of doorways so that the light moved, not abruptly, but by increments. As the interior architecture was stripped to its essentials, the details that remained, notably the ironwork stair handrails and balusters, grew increasingly more refined, as did the house's simple set of materials, little more than metal, plaster, and wood. Once I found the project's rhythm and the rich vein of inspiration stood revealed, the design coalesced quickly, virtually within a matter of days. We were all excited, enthused—and then the project entered a state of suspended animation.

Six years later, the house emerged from hibernation at a moment when my practice had expanded and the time I had available to contemplate an idea had compressed. And so it was interesting and instructive to be tapped on the shoulder by my younger, surely less busy, and perhaps purer self. As the largely unaltered scheme transformed into a built reality, I was pleased to discover how effectively our efforts at simplification and emphasis on volume played out, how the few refined details and rich materiality were intensified. Most of all I was surprised by the quality of the light: how it moved through the house in a warm, golden transit; tumbled down from the upper floors with the random elegance of a waterfall; how it compelled the palpable to recede and drew the temporal to the fore. To be sure, the house was a house, all 6,500 square feet of it. But the story it told was one of motion, time, and—above all—light.

Recently I had occasion to revisit the place, a decade or so after its completion, and I made two further discoveries. The first was how effectively the landscaping

has come into its own. When we were preparing for construction, we had to excavate a hillside rather severely to capture enough level ground on which to build. As this left us without much to look at, I was inspired to create a tableau of monumental stairs leading to nowhere as a substitute for a more conventionally picturesque view. With the passage of time, this gambit has settled elegantly into the slope at the site's rear to form an appropriate setting for the architecture. My frequent collaborator, landscape architect John Howard, had much to do with this maturation. Elaborating on my original idea with elegance and restraint, John added a terminus of curvilinear clipped hedges, which give the stairs a focal point and increase their resemblance to a classical amphitheater. Now they possess the character of a ruin—a memento mori—a quality that lends a romantic aspect to the view.

My other happy discovery was how gracefully the building has accepted its interior design elements, which remained unfinished the previous time I visited. My clients are as appreciative of simplicity in the applied arts as in architecture, and so they decorated the rooms sparingly with exquisitely beautiful objects and furnishings that added just enough to each space. That, for me, is one of the most valuable lessons the project teaches: the simplicity of the building allows the folks who live there to use it as a canvas, to great—and, I hope, lasting—effect.

And there are other lessons. With an appreciation of the economy with which the house was realized, my staff and I have begun producing fewer drawings—making the ones we create comprehensive and correct, but not overthinking the detail at the expense of form. I am paying closer attention to the ways in which the passage of light can bring a static building to life and set it in sublime motion. Most usefully, I am studying the DNA of the Knoxville project, looking for those instinctive epiphanies that my younger self stumbled upon, so that I can marshal them in a conscious way.

We learn from our mistakes. But success can be a fine teacher as well, especially if it springs from something pure and authentic deep within us. And hopefully in the process the magic is not lost—that's the eternal challenge.

OPPOSITE: The terminus at the top of the amphitheater stairs, planted with ornamental grasses. The entirety of the landscape element invests the property with a sense of history and provides a powerful visual element in what had been an otherwise unexceptional setting.

RIGHT: The foyer terminates in a small outdoor sitting area off the side garden. The stonework on the low wall uses reclaimed rocks from an old barn structure. OVERLEAF: In the family room, I eliminated the mantelpiece and used the soft lines of the stucco to frame the Rumford fireplace; also absent are baseboards and moldings, and the walls are roughly troweled plaster. The owner designed the interiors in collaboration with interior designer Monique Gibson. PAGES 150–151: The absence of baseboards, the textured finishes, transformed the walls into canvases that showcase the simple decorative tableaux.

ABOVE: The upstairs loggia. OPPOSITE: The downstairs media room, off the lower terrace. OVERLEAF: I found the inspiration for the scalloped design of the stair in Italy, rendered in stone. The ultrasimple hand-hammered steel rail makes a greater impression given the absence of such detail elsewhere in the house.

ABOVE: A view of the garage. OPPOSITE: The foyer and
mudroom. In all of the house's precincts, I emphasized
mass, light, and space over architectural detail.

The lightly figured black
soapstone counter and
backsplash with an oil finish
make the simple kitchen
feel luxurious. The owner
found the copper lanterns.

Simplicity, Chopin observed, is the hardest thing, the final thing—and the objective we all pursued for this house.

OPPOSITE: In the kitchen, a dish pantry discovered by my clients in France.

RIGHT: A capacious steel-framed window opens up to a garden view from the downstairs study. OVERLEAF: The living room is the repository of the house's major architectural details, in the form of a reclaimed mantelpiece and a pulled-plaster cove crown molding.

PREVIOUS SPREAD: When interiors are reduced to planes, textures, and simple materials, the few interventions—whether architectural or artistic— stand out in high relief. RIGHT: The master bedroom with an antique mirror above the fireplace.

ABOVE: A bedroom in the guest wing. OPPOSITE: The upstairs enclosed loggia, in the back of the house above the porch.

ABOVE: The master bedroom. OPPOSITE: The master bath with a glass wall that opens onto the courtyard. OVERLEAF: The hand-scraped wood trim atop this curvaceous headboard complements the wall and contrasts with the fine upholstery.

ABOVE AND OPPOSITE: Guest room details.
OVERLEAF: The courtyard off the master bath.

LOW-COUNTRY PLANTATION

I first visited Palmetto Bluff, which is inshore of Daufuskie and Hilton Head Islands in South Carolina, some fifteen years ago, when it was an almost entirely undeveloped expanse of piney woods. Its exceptional beauty, I could see, derived from a unique set of circumstances. It was, on the one hand, possessed of typical low-country charms: the marsh was mysterious and ever changing, a pristine, prelapsarian landscape rich in bird, mammal, and marine life. Yet there was high ground as well, which gave you long views, incredible sunsets, and gigantic live oak trees that ringed the shoreline. I was properly stunned, and though the area had years to go before anything could be built on it, that singular combination of low and high country remained indelibly etched in my memory.

A decade or so later, I returned to find a handsomely constructed, appropriately modest country town that made Palmetto Bluff habitable without erasing its natural charms. I had been invited back by my clients, who'd laid hands on an unusual parcel on the outskirts of the development, roughly one hundred by three hundred feet. The property had much to recommend it, in particular the east-facing views: there were magnificent sunrises, of course, but dusk was equally dramatic. When the sun slipped below the horizon, it created incredible highlights on the treetops, which then seemed to blaze against the darkening sky. These charms, however, came with a challenge. As the property was close to the water, the land was marshy and difficult to build upon.

To bring the house up to bluff height, I borrowed a gambit I'd seen in the historic manors of Savannah, where you find partial floors at street level and the main living areas on the piano nobile, one flight up. To achieve the same effect, we constructed retaining walls and filled in the front yard, so that from the street the house appears to be a one-and-a-half-story residence, and when you approach you hardly notice the gradual incline. But it is there, and that extra space enabled me to elevate the main floor by some fifteen feet. The garages, media area, gym, and storage spaces are semi-submerged underneath, and a screened cooking porch is

OPPOSITE: A view into the wife's study from the foyer. The space is finished in painted wood paneling and boasts a lively chevron floor and a coffered ceiling styled as a circle and four quadrants. OVERLEAF: The rear elevation, with columns of limewashed brick on the lower level that taper into double wooden columns above. At the top, a long copper shed dormer contains the master bedroom and bath.

open to the landscape on the rear facade. This bit of legerdemain gives the house a more discreet public profile—and it also dramatically improved the view.

My clients, who'd moved to Palmetto Bluff from Louisiana, had a firm notion of what they wanted stylistically: a traditional low-country classical Southern house, but not one like their grandparents might have built. Instead they sought a place that spoke to the times, and to them. This manifested itself in the architecture, both within and without. On the rear elevation, which exposes the house's full height, I began with limewashed brick pilasters on the bottom level, then split them into double columns, constructed from wood, on the main floor. From the ground to the entablature, these have the precise proportions of classical columns elongated to a two-story height, and there is nothing filling the spaces between them but screening. The outcome is a contemporary take on the local tradition of big white columns on a massive white plantation-style house—a deconstructed play on historic low-country classical architecture rather than a literal replication.

On the inside, I subverted expectations with a plan that begins as the acme of tradition, then becomes progressively more contemporary. The front door opens onto a classical foyer, flanked by his-and-hers studies; the foyer then transforms into a dining hall/circulation space leading to an open plan kitchen/family room—dispensing with an old-style parlor entirely—terminating in a long screen porch. By progressively dematerializing the interior architecture, I was able to part with historic convention and create rooms reflective of the way young families live in the modern world.

I am pleased with the house's comfortable synthesis of historic contextualism and the spatial sensibilities of the present day. But I am especially proud of the project's demonstration that, architecturally, one need not be enslaved by the restrictions of a flood zone. The functional requirements imposed by the threat of a hurricane do not preclude a well-designed house—and that's as important a statement as any design can make.

OPPOSITE: A detail of the wife's study reveals reclaimed glass panes in the corner cabinet—one of four that transform the space into an octagon. OVERLEAF: The view from the front door through the foyer—her study to the right, his to the left—to the dining room.

The dining room actually occupies a transitional space—an enclosed porch-cum-hallway connecting the family room and library wings of the house. The main stair sits eccentrically behind the table.

The iconography of history and context, combined with the spatial and programmatic needs of today, together form the foundation of the new Southern home.

OPPOSITE: Michelle Smith created the house's interiors, which mix antique and contemporary furnishings with lively textiles and intriguing, detailed tableaux. OVERLEAF: An archway separates the kitchen from the family room; the first-floor back porch is to the right, the dining room to the left.

OPPOSITE: In the mudroom, the beamed ceiling supports the landing of the main stair. ABOVE: The butler's pantry, which connects to the mudroom (to the left at the far end of the space).

PREVIOUS SPREAD: The wife's bath features hand-painted wallpaper
and a stone tub. ABOVE AND OPPOSITE: The children's rooms, tucked
inside the roofline, feature exposed painted timbers and floors.

A painted floor enlivens
the upstairs screen porch
off the family room.

A ROOM
WITH A VIEW

My second home, in rural Georgia, has been described in many ways, and I must say that it inspires a certain pride to have one's (somewhat eccentric) abode characterized so imaginatively. Its basic form is simple: a twenty-by-twenty-foot stone tower, some seventy feet high, with a traditional Southern wraparound porch, built from unfinished timbers sawn from yellow pine, at the base. Perhaps the most amusing evocation of this object that I've heard is that it's a San Gimignano *torre* dressed in a hoopskirt. But the place's most authentic ancestor is the so-called shot tower, which back in the days of the muzzle-loader was used for making bullets: people would build a tower with a furnace up top, melt lead, pour it through a sieve, and let it drop into a bucket far below—a process that produced near-perfect spheres.

The precise elucidation of typology, I suppose, is never easy. The most important thing to know is when you get up to the very top, an open aerie with 360-degree views and a soothing breeze even on the hottest days, it's an awfully nice place to be.

The house found its form opportunistically, in that I was in essence following an idea, not entirely certain where it might lead. The first time I walked the land, the previous owner and I were quail hunting, and we flushed a covey on the precise spot where the house stands today. A large mound of stones, tossed there over the decades by farmers, occupied the site, and it occurred to me that I might use material from the property to construct a rustic structure. This notion braided with the fact that the acreage, though substantial, had no essential amenity—no sizable body of water or picturesque view. I postulated that if I could get up high enough, I'd be able to sight Pine Mountain, and *that* thought connected with a childhood memory of climbing the silos on my grandfather's dairy farm and the great views that awaited me at their tops.

So, I thought, why *not* build a great big stone tower in the middle of nowhere?

I drew the structure, more as inspiration than a specific construction document. That's because I actually had no firm idea about how high I was going to go. The way it worked was, we'd build a floor and then I'd get up on a tall ladder and see how the view might look from the next elevation. When I arrived at what I assumed would be the top—the atelier above the master bedroom—I decided to go just a bit higher: I could see the mountain ridge and knew that with another dozen or so feet I'd be able to see over it. There is pleasure to be had from

OPPOSITE: My home as I originally envisioned it. OVERLEAF: The entrance to the tower is at right. The two stone steps lead to the pool terrace.

an open-ended vertical ascent, the conclusion of which is determined only by a sudden, special feeling in one's soul. It is a pleasure usually denied an architect, who must adhere to a client's budget and program, but in this case I was able to grasp it.

A curious thing about the relationship between a structure and its surroundings: when you first see the land, you can't imagine putting anything on it, and then after it's been fitted with an object, you can't imagine the land without it. That, I think, is what makes my home feel particularly Italian—in one's mind, it is difficult to separate the landscape of Tuscany from its towers. Given this indispensable interdependency, I devoted much thought to how the house might connect to the land and vice versa: not only how they looked together, but also the ways in which each could be a vehicle for experiencing the other, as well as mediating between interior and exterior space.

This is most evident in the handling of that wooden hoopskirt, the porch. I kept the differences between the three conditions—indoors, covered, and fully exposed—relatively slender, so that one experiences a natural progression between them. One is never entirely a part of the landscape or the architecture but can slip between the two (unless, of course, you go way out or way in). As the porch is what might be described as the South's comfort zone—the place where people become relaxed enough to widen the doors of perception—I gave much consideration to the view, especially from the side that overlooks the pool and the expanse of loosely enclosed lawn beyond it. Originally, that lawn terminated not far from the water, but after a year or so, I extended it another fifty yards. In part, I wanted to give my boys enough room to play football. But it also felt important to create a precinct that *belonged* to the house yet was big enough to enable one to *behold* the house. Being able to embrace the tower in all its fullness, on its own turf, as it were, highlights both its mastery of and subservience to the natural world—an interdependence that is so much a part of our region.

In the introduction to this book, I declared that the tower house represented a personal embrace of one of my own most cherished professional beliefs: that a great idea all but ensures a great residence, and it is better to adjust oneself to that idea's eccentricities than to violate its purity. I cited, by way of example, the fact that the master bath is two levels below the bedroom, necessitating a lot of stair-climbing but preserving the three-sided view. I'll stand by that philosophy of practice, but I have to admit that, several years after the fact, I slipped a second bathroom onto the stair landing behind my sleeping quarters. I tell people that it's a reflection of the Piranesian idea of the interesting ruin, the fragment that provokes speculation about the vanity of human ambition, and the little five-by-eight-foot cypress-clad bump-out on the tower's side does enrich the narrative. Better still, it makes la dolce vita in my corner of the South that much sweeter.

PAGES 206–207: The house has been compared to an Italian tower dressed in a Southern hoopskirt. PREVIOUS SPREAD: Its precincts include a pool off the porch and, loosely enclosed by a low wall, an expanse of lawn amidst the ungoverned natural surroundings. OPPOSITE: Another of my impressionistic renderings.

Rather than childproofing the porch enclosure, I stacked firewood under the rail. It keeps kids from falling off, and the ends of the logs are nicely in sympathy with the texture of the stone walls.

I clad the living room in old cypress logs reclaimed from Southern rivers. The pattern of the ceiling—an overlapping series of octagons—was originally detailed by a lumber company for use on a beach club, and I loved it so much, I used a small portion in my own home. It's a surprising moment of formality in an otherwise informal house.

ABOVE: The exterior stone and the interior cypress meet in the stair to the upper floor. OPPOSITE: In the kitchen, my well-curated, well-cured cast-iron frying pans. I bagged the turkey above the door to the pantry on a hunting trip.

The spare chairs on the wall
were built aboard the
icebound ship of a polar explorer,
using walrus gut for the seats.
I like them because they are
light and add a nice sense of
decoration—and they're useful.
OVERLEAF: A child's "dorm
room" in the tower.

PREVIOUS SPREAD: The home studio I keep sits directly above the master bedroom and is open to it in the middle—when I'm in bed I look up and think I should be working, and when I'm at the drafting table, I look down and wish I was asleep. RIGHT: A corner fireplace in the master bedroom between two of the three expansive window walls.

ABOVE: Behind the bed in the master bedroom, a curtain conceals the stair. OPPOSITE: This bathroom is two flights below the bedroom, but as compensation there's a superlative view from the tub.

PREVIOUS SPREAD: A view to the pond past the guest cottage with its deliberately precarious-looking stone foundation and cedar-tree column. RIGHT: The entrance to the guest cottage is, you might say, touched by rustic grandeur with its rough pilasters and stone lions guarding the rock stoop.

PREVIOUS SPREAD, LEFT: The back door of the guest cottage features a portrait of the main house rendered in pierced tin. (I'd like to say that I shot it out with my .22 pistol, but the truth is it was made with a hammer, a nail, and a banged-up thumb.) PREVIOUS SPREAD, RIGHT: The kitchen is cabinet-free. ABOVE AND OPPOSITE: The inexpensive plywood walls of the guest bedrooms are finished with a milk-wash paint. OVERLEAF: Evening: the best time of day.

ACKNOWLEDGMENTS

Acknowledging the many talented people who have contributed to this book is no small task. First, I must say that Malissa Peace (who recommended Jill Cohen) started me off on this rewarding journey. Jill was unsure of the content and how gardens and architecture would translate into a book, but quickly found a strong direction after visiting one of my projects in Atlanta. From that time on, the leadership of the project was on sure footing.

Jill brought a host of remarkable individuals (and not a little hand-holding) to our project, notably Gemma and Andrew Ingalls, our primary photographers. As a husband-and-wife team, they brought a special set of creative eyes suitable to capturing the subtlety and material textures our work employs.

Marc Kristal, my co-writer, insisted on visiting me at my farm, arriving directly from the canyons of Manhattan and immersing himself in a Southern landscape, far away from the bustle of the city. He sat on my porch and rocked and talked about my arcane design philosophy with such enthusiasm that I myself began to believe in it!

I do not wish to forget others on the team, such as Doug Turshen and Steve Turner, as well as Kathleen Jayes at Rizzoli, all of whom pushed the pages through the visual and editorial processes.

I would also like to acknowledge my staff, which forms the engine behind which all else is pulled—particularly Matthew Welden, who coordinated all of the photo shoots with our gracious clients and helped me focus on the myriad book-related tasks we were asked to perform over the last several years.

My family and friends participated in this effort by giving me the time and support to take on the travel and meetings required to build the book. My two boys, Hugh and Harrison, have chosen careers in design and architecture; as they have watched their dad with both interest and amusement, they have rekindled in the old man the enthusiasm of youth. Their journeys will produce their own brand of design, tailored to a new and vibrant generation. Thanks for being the spark that ignites my path.

To one and all: As I think about our time together, I am reminded that the process was fun—and was an adventure in discovering the essence of our work, one that allowed me to see the future with new eyes.

Thank you all for your good work,

Keith

First published in the United States of America in 2017
by Rizzoli International Publications, Inc.
300 Park Avenue South
New York, NY 10010
www.rizzoliusa.com

2017 2018 2019 2020 / 10 9 8 7 6 5 4 3 2 1

Distributed in the U.S. trade by Random House, New York

Printed in China

All photos by Andrew and Gemma Ingalls except pages 48-49 by Mali Azima;
pages 74-87 and 112-133 by Simon Upton; and pages 53-73 by Erica George Dines.

Design by Doug Turshen with Steve Turner

ISBN-13: 978-0-8478-5873-6
Library of Congress Control Number: 2016953378